# The Best Wholesaling Book Ever

ALL IN Entrepreneurs

**Authors: Carlos Reyes, Sal Shakir & Alex Saenz**

*Written By: Carson Jones*

# CONTENTS

# INTRODUCTION

## The Best Wholesaling Book Ever

Aspiring entrepreneurs ask us often, "how do I get rich?" Instead, the question should be, "how do I become wealthy?" Rich is fleeting. Rich may help you purchase a fancy car or a watch that feeds your ego. Yet, real wealth happens over time, and if your goal is to build wealth, you need a vehicle to get you there. What if we told you that over 90% of the world's millionaires all had one thing in common? They made their fortunes in real estate.

Real estate has been around for generations, and until we are living in the sky or on another planet, real estate isn't going anywhere. Even if Elon Musk can take us to Mars, we will need somewhere to live. Real estate has been around forever, and it isn't going anywhere, anytime soon. Real estate is a tried and true industry, with an almost guaranteed growth trajectory over time.

The difference between real estate and many of the other wealth-building industries is the low barrier to entry. If you have an excellent idea for groundbreaking technology, your idea is only as good as the money you can raise. If you want to create wealth through traditional professions like a doctor or lawyer, you are tasked with years of schooling and debt that will take years to recover from. If you can predict the future, you might be able to guess which industry will become the next cryptocurrency, cannabis, or diet fad that will change the world. For the rest of us, there is a simple blueprint that created wealth for us, the people around us, and millions of others before us. That blueprint starts with real estate because you don't need a fancy education, you can start with little to no money, and there are hundreds of ways to get paid if you are a hardworking, creative entrepreneur.

While many of those ways require working capital, we had no money when we got started in real estate. Just as many of the people reading this book, we came from nothing. However, we all had something far more valuable than money. We had the work ethic, desire, and a will to succeed that couldn't be deterred.

That's when we discovered the art of wholesaling, and over the last five years, we turned our desire to succeed into a thriving real estate operation with over 100+ employees. We've been able to generate millions of dollars without taking the risk of owning properties, which has allowed us to create financial freedom for ourselves and our families.

Wholesaling real estate is a vehicle that allows aspiring entrepreneurs to land high commission deals without putting any of their money at risk. Wholesaling isn't a get rich quick scheme, and before we go any further, you must know what kind of work ethic is required to succeed in this industry.

We have done all of the heavy lifting for you. When we started in real estate, there was no blueprint that we could follow. We spent years researching and perfecting the strategies laid out in this book. We have also spent millions of dollars testing these strategies so that you don't have to make the same mistakes that we made.

Everyone sees the luxurious lives and financial freedom we have built today. People see the Lamborghinis, watches, trips, and estates we have today, but they don't see the sacrifice we made to get there. We started in a 250 sq. foot room with no air conditioning. We worked every day from 5 am – 2 am with no mentorship or direction. We sacrificed hobbies, family time, friendships, entertainment, and even our health because we knew what we had to do if we wanted to be successful.

We share this not to scare you, but to inspire you. If you want to live the life of your dreams, you will need to make major sacrifices. We want you to know what to expect as you begin your journey towards success.

## What is wholesaling?

Wholesaling is the art of finding off-market properties at a discounted price and then contracting that property with the owner.

Remember, you are a real estate entrepreneur. Not a realtor or a real estate investor.

As a real estate entrepreneur, your only job is to help people solve problems. Your work ethic and your ability to problem-solve are what create value and ultimately gets you paid. The only reason a property owner would agree to sell at a discounted price is if you can solve a problem significant enough to help them out of a current situation. If you have any questions throughout this book or want to learn more about wholesaling, check out all of our resources at allinnation.com.

## Why would someone agree to a discounted price?

A traditional real estate deal doesn't happen quickly and requires your home to be able to pass inspections along the way. If a seller is looking to get top dollar for their home, there is a long, expensive, and sometimes painful process they must go through.

A homeowner may not have time to wait, or maybe they don't have money to make home repairs. In many situations, people just want to sell their home for a fair cash offer and move on with their lives. This is what you would describe as a motivated seller.

**These situations could include:**

- Finalizing a messy divorce
- Back taxes are too high, and they risk losing their home/foreclosure
- An inherited home when a loved one passes/probate
- An urgent job relocation
- A disgruntled landlord that needs an excuse to move on from a bad tenant
- Damages that weren't covered by insurance
- Repairs that they can't afford to fix
- Downsizing

- Job loss/financial hardship

All of these issues would make it difficult for the owner to sell the home the traditional route. Your ability to find those motivated sellers, and solve their problems is the reason you can command high commissions without ever owning the property.

**How can I make a purchase offer on a property with no money and no credit?**

The reason why cash or credit isn't needed is that your job as a real estate entrepreneur is to solve problems. By solving problems for the motivated seller, you also create assets that real estate investors/fix & flippers are looking for. Once you agree on a price with your seller, you place the property under contract at that price. Your goal then is to find an end buyer/cash buyer for a higher price, and you will walk away with the difference. Example: You put a property under contract for $150,000. You assign the contract to the cash buyer for $170,000, and you walk away with the $20,000 difference!! The goal is to do this over and over and over again.

**Why would a real estate investor pay a higher price?**

Real estate investors are always looking for more inventory, and they will also make plenty of money after renovating the property. Keep in mind, real estate investors are reactive. They sit around and wait for people like you, a real estate entrepreneur, to bring them deals. Remember, you are finding properties that they desperately want just by being proactive. Most of the properties you find are not available on any traditional marketplaces. While the motivated seller didn't have the time or money to get top dollar for their property, the real estate investor does. Here is an example deal that will better explain the situation:

**ARV (Actual Retail Value):** $300,000

**Agreement Price:** $175,000

**Investor Price:** $195,000

**Agency Fees/Closing Costs:** $21,000 (7%)

**Investor Repairs:** $35,000

**Investor Profit:** $49,000

**Your Profit:** $20,000

In this scenario, the homeowner had fallen behind on mortgage payments. They had just received a notice that their home would go into foreclosure within the next 30 days. Instead of losing the house to foreclosure, you can offer them a cash purchase of $175,000.

The real estate investor understands they only need to put $35,000 into overall repairs to bring the property value to $300,000. The investor pays $195,000 for the home, and you make $20,000 as a finders fee. After the investor repairs the property, the investor makes $49,000 once the home sells for top dollar, minus agency fees, and closing costs of 7%.

This is the art of the deal that makes real estate investing so rewarding. In this situation, everyone wins. The motivated seller was facing foreclosure and risked getting nothing for their home. Instead, they walk away with $175,000 to cover the cost of their mortgage. You make $20,000 for your hard work, and the real estate investor makes $49,000 from the deal. Everyone wins, and you risked nothing besides your sweat equity and time. You are paid handsomely for your work, and you are free to move on to your next deal.

Once you know how to find the deals and have a list of real estate investors that purchase properties, you can replicate this process while continuing to collect profits. The process is simple but complicated. These deals are not well known, and many of the motivated sellers you are looking for, are unaware that you exist. Levels of motivation also vary. Somebody could just be starting to fall behind on payments, or they may be convinced that they can still get top dollar for their home. We have developed a tried and true system for finding motivated sellers and closing more deals. For more information or guidance on this exact process, visit us at allinnation.com.

**What are the requirements to become a Real Estate Entrepreneur?**

You don't need a college education, you don't need a real estate license, and you don't need any money. However, you do need to make a decision that success is not an option. You must go all in and be honest with yourself about what it means to be ALL IN. You must be willing to sacrifice time with family, spend long hours perfecting your craft, spend months marketing without results and take massive action along the way to your success. You have to eliminate all of your excuses, remove the mental programming of your past. Ignore the naysayers that question your ambitions and persevere through thousands of no's on the way towards your success.

**You are one deal away from changing your life!!**

Once you do land your first deal, you need the discipline to remain poor and delay gratification. Focus on expanding and reinvesting back into your business. After all, you are starting this journey to become wealthy, not rich. Wealth is a journey worth pursuing, and real estate is the vehicle that will take you there. However, it won't happen overnight, and it won't happen unless you go ALL IN.

# CHAPTER 1

# ALL IN ENTREPRENEURS: Who Are We?

*"It's easy for you to say, you are a millionaire."*

All too often, we discover someone after the darkest hours of their lives, after the years of struggle and sacrifice. If this book is the first you're hearing of us, then you might be saying, "It's easy for you to say, you are a millionaire." Things didn't start like this, and when we say we have been in your shoes before, all three of us came from nothing. So, who are we and how did we get here?

## Carlos Reyes

After coming to America illegally as a child, Carlos Reyes is the definition of the American dream. However, it never came easy, and he watched his family struggle for much of his childhood and young adult life. Carlos worked as a child bagging groceries for minimal pay and surviving off tips before he decided to help his family by selling bread door-to-door.

Carlos still recalls the days he and his brother would knock on doors, hoping to sell enough bread to allow his family to move to the U.S.

Even after saving enough money to come to the U.S., Carlos watched his mother struggle to get by. Times were so tough; when they moved to America, they stayed in a friend's hallway surrounded by other tenants because they couldn't afford a better place to live. His mother was his inspiration. She worked long hours at multiple jobs, making low wages, just to make sure their family could survive.

When Carlos was old enough to work, he would do everything in his power to help his family. Carlos took positions in construction, odd jobs, and even worked a full-time job at Best Buy while discovering his passion in real estate. He then decided to quit his 14-year corporate job in

2015 to pursue the dream of building his own Real Estate investment company.

With the help of his partner Sal Shakir, the company has scaled quickly to be a real estate powerhouse, consistently producing six figures every single month in multiple markets. Carlos also owns another 25 businesses. Carlos recently purchased a 1-acre estate in Glendale, Arizona, where he, his wife, and two daughters reside. Carlos and his family are now truly living the American Dream.

**Sal Shakir**

When Sal Shakir immigrated to the U.S. at age 15, he had already lived an entire lifetime of hardships. Growing up in Iraq, Shakir grew up in an actual war zone. There were break-ins, bombings, and his father was shot. They sacrificed and risked everything to come to America, and when they made it to the U.S., things were far from easy.

His father worked hard to support his family, but Sal knew he had to help as well. Sal could barely speak English at the time, so he started by working odd jobs to help his family survive.

At one point, they nearly had to sell their home, and Sal wasn't willing to let that happen. Sal would go to school earlier than the other students so he could leave early and work his odd jobs to help his family. Sal worked as a painter, plumber, door knocker, and anything else he could find to support his family.

Eventually, Shakir got into the business of selling and flipping cars. He built great relationships with wholesalers and the dealerships learning how to buy and sell cars. His first major entrepreneurial venture was opening his own car dealership. He was able to eventually able to save $3000 before using that to help his mother pay off her credit card bill, taking him back to nothing.

After months of more hard work, Shakir was able to purchase a property that had recently been damaged by a fire. He knew he was handy enough to fix the house himself, which was the beginning of his career in real estate. Eventually, after renting the home to tenants, he finally decided to sell the property.

Shortly after selling the property, he met his now business partner Carlos Reyes, who had become successful in wholesaling real estate. This industry was similar to what

Shakir was already doing with his car dealership. After just selling his first property, his entrepreneurial instincts told him he had to go for it.

Fast forward to today, Shakir is living the American dream as a successful entrepreneur. National Cash Offer is one of the largest real estate companies in the U.S. based in Phoenix, Arizona. He employs hundreds of people, and many of those are his family members and closest friends.

### Alex Saenz

At the age of 18, Alex was left searching for answers. His parents had just separated, and he was dead broke, living with his father in a trailer park. He had been accepted into college but had no financial backing and no support from his family. Alex was lost and spent that year in a very dark place.

Once Alex found real estate, he knew it was his vehicle for success, but it wouldn't happen quickly. In May 2015, Alex decided to forego college to pursue real estate. In the first few months, he spent time learning but couldn't land his first deal.

He was forced to move in with friends; he went into debt and had many deals fall through along the way.

It took Alex over nine months before he finally landed his first deal. Instead of celebrating, he continued to invest every dollar into his business. Along the way, he met Sal Shakir and Carlos Reyes. The three like-minded individuals continued to run their real estate businesses separately but started multiple other businesses together before eventually starting ALL IN Entrepreneurs.

Alex is now a multi-millionaire and owns over 15 businesses, mostly within the real estate industry.

If you want to hear more about our stories, who we are and what we do, visit allinnation.com.

## Now it's your turn

Do our stories sound familiar? Our stories may be similar to something you are currently going through. Maybe you lack the education to get a traditional job. Perhaps you are working at a job but know you want more out of life. You may be struggling to take care of your family or just struggling to find your true passion and vision for your life. If you are reading this thinking, yes, yes, and yes, just know that you are not alone. Between the three of us, we have faced every adversity you are about to face. We have been through every struggle, every failure, and every test of faith.

When we started in the real estate industry, there were very few resources that explained how this business worked. Real estate entrepreneurship wasn't glamorous, and it wasn't filled with experts that could guide us along the way. Today, there are more "gurus" than ever, and the misinformation is more dangerous than having no information. Real estate is a beautiful industry, filled with opportunities. However, if you don't know the right way to find, negotiate, and close deals, you will waste valuable time along your journey.

We have spent over 5+ years growing and scaling our companies. Now, our goal is to give you our all-access blueprint that we wish we had when we got started in real estate. Take this as your A-Z guide on landing your first deal. Before you start on your real estate journey, start by looking in the mirror and making a decision.

## CHAPTER 2

# ALL IN Success Formula

Every great journey starts with a decision and a conversation about what you want out of life. We hear excuses every day from aspiring entrepreneurs in every industry that says they are working hard, but not landing deals or not getting the results they want. When we look deeper into their work ethic, they want success, but they aren't willing to sacrifice what it takes to become successful. Success isn't a by chance occurrence. Success is an ALL-IN decision that eliminates all excuses and backup plans.

**Burn your ships**

In 1519, Captain Hernán Cortés landed in Veracruz with a fleet of ships and 600 men ready to conquer the Aztec empire. Upon arrival, Cortés ordered his men to burn the ships. Why would he do that? Cortés knew that if they had a backup plan, they would ultimately fail. At the first sign of danger, some of the men may retreat to the ships for safety. Burning the ships symbolized that there were no other options. The men would either conquer the Aztec empire, or they would all die.

Two years later, Cortés succeeded in his conquest.

Entrepreneurship is far from a life or death conquest, but there is a lesson here. Once you commit to go all-in, you must eliminate all of your backup plans. If you are deciding that success is the only option, you must eliminate all other options. If you are thinking to yourself, "I'll give real estate a try for 60 days, and if it doesn't work out, I'll go get a job," then you have already lost. Real estate will test you every day, and when things get hard, you need the burn the ships mentality to push you through the difficult times on your way to success.

Remember Alex Saenz's story? It took Alex over 9+ months to land his first deal. During that period, he had multiple deals that appeared finalized, only to fall through at the last minute. If Alex had a backup plan, it would have been easy for him to run to those excuses and say, "I'm so unlucky, real estate just isn't for me." Instead, when he decided he wasn't going to college, Alex burned his ships, leaving him no other options but to succeed.

Once you make that decision and burn your ships, you must be ready to sacrifice what it takes to achieve that success.

**Start with you: Mindset**

Growing up, we are all programmed to become part of the societal "system." We are taught to go to school, get a good job, get married, have kids, work until we retire and die. That's the lifestyle that millions of people subconsciously choose every day. Once you decide that success is the only option, you have to be prepared to battle your subconscious programming.

What are the stories you tell yourself daily? Do you believe you can succeed? Once you make the decision, you need to start unraveling all of your preexisting fears or doubts of failure because every step of the way, you will have to answer questions that will further test your level of commitment.

The first questions will come from yourself and your inner voice.

- Can I actually do this?
- Is real estate right for me?
- Can I quit my job?
- Will my family suffer from this decision?
- Is it the right time to go all-in?
- Nobody in my family has ever achieved anything significant, what makes me so special?

## Fear, fear, fear

Every entrepreneur has faced these same doubts and fears. These are just a few of the questions you will ask yourself both internally and externally when times get tough. Your inner conviction and confidence must be greater than your subconscious doubts because only one side can win. When you find yourself in the darkest moments on your journey, which voice will win out? Start breaking down your old programming and input new, effective programming that will push you through these difficult moments.

## How do you change your programming?

Have you ever heard the phrase, "you are the sum of the 5 friends you spend the most time with?" The number 5 is relative, but your surroundings directly impact your results.

Let's start with this example:

You have decided to start your journey into real estate, and your excitement level is at an all-time high. You see successful entrepreneurs living the lifestyle you want to live. With conviction, you start telling all of your family and friends that you are going to be a successful real estate entrepreneur.

Your friends and family genuinely care about you. However, unless you already have highly successful friends, very few of them can relate to the lofty goals and expectations you have set for yourself. You will hear phrases like "Why are you chasing these huge goals?" or "You know you can't actually do that" or our personal favorite "That sounds illegal." It's not that they don't want the best for you; they are merely justifying to themselves why they themselves are not successful. This is especially true when you are attempting to break multiple generations of family curses. People subconsciously want to justify why they didn't achieve more, and the best way they know-how is by giving you the same advice that they received.

They want you to play it safe because that's what they did. When this happens, ask yourself, "Do I want to live the life of the person giving me this advice?" Even if that person is someone you love deeply, you should ask yourself this question and be very honest with yourself about the answer.

Now let's say the five people you spend the most time with are entrepreneurs that have achieved what you want to achieve. They have been through the tough times and fought through them on their way to success. There is a strong transferrable belief about being present with those that have already achieved what you want to achieve. The advice is essential because they can help you navigate issues and obstacles you will face. However, it's the belief in the possibility of success that becomes most powerful.

Before 1954, it was believed by doctors that if you ran a sub-four-minute mile, your heart would physically explode out of your chest. Many athletes had tried and failed, leaving very little faith that it was even possible. Then Roger Bannister came along and became the first person to break the four-minute mile. His heart didn't explode, and he broke the mental barrier for everyone else. Now, people knew that a sub-four-minute mile was possible because it had been accomplished. In the year following Bannisters' accomplishment, dozens of other people also shattered the four-minute mile pace, and now it is common practice for most professional runners.

Why did something that seemed impossible, suddenly become achievable… BELIEF! If Roger Bannister would have taken the advice from loved ones or colleagues, perhaps he would have never even attempted to push through that four-minute pace. Once he accomplished the feat, others now believed it was possible. Believing you can achieve something is necessary before you can achieve it. By surrounding yourself with people who have accomplished your dreams, it builds a sense of belief for what is possible.

You need to surround yourself with other Roger Bannisters. Seek advice via mentorship, podcasts, and books of those that have been where you want to be. Start going to meetups, conferences, and network with individuals that have completed the journey. After reading this book, you will understand that the art of landing your first deal is a relatively simple process. It's the belief and perseverance that will make or break your success.

If you need a strong support system that can keep you accountable, while helping you shift your shift your mental programming, check out our mentorship programs at allinnation.com.

## Commitment & sacrifice

If you have made the decision to succeed and have decided to burn your proverbial ships, then there will be sacrifices you must make when success is your only option. If the tone of this section sounds intense, that is the point. You will only become successful when you want to succeed as badly as you want to breathe. If you are reading this book thinking, "Wow this is intense, I'm not sure if I'm ready for this," then you likely are not. Turn on Netflix, meet your friends at happy hour, and continue on your journey of comfort.

If you are reading this book thinking, "I'm ready to make all of the changes," then prepare yourself, because it's going to get uncomfortable. If you can make these sacrifices and success becomes your number one priority, all of your life's dreams await.

We already discussed the power of proximity and the importance of the people you surround yourself with. This may mean cutting out some friendships or learning to block out the poor advice you are getting from your aunt Karen. You don't need these distractions or limiting beliefs on your journey to success. Your family and friends love you, but they may be an enemy to your success.

It is also time to cancel the Netflix and cable membership because every free minute you have will be diving into your burning desire for success. Netflix will be there in a few years once you have built a huge operation and have four sales associates that help free up your time. For now, you need to eliminate distractions and spend every waking minute developing yourself and your business. The time you had spent watching Netflix becomes the time you are reading books and watching real estate courses that will help you develop your skills while reprogramming your mind. Your friends and family will resist the change at first, but they won't mind at all when you're picking up the check at dinner a year from now.

**Understand your WHY**

Up until this point, have you ever stopped to consider your WHY? Why do you want to be successful in the first place? Is it ego-driven because you want to prove something to others? Is it because you want to get rich and buy fancy cars?

Superficial whys will only lead to short-term highs and fleeting levels of success. Once your friends see you as successful, then what? Once you buy that fancy Rolex, then what? Your why must go deeper than that, or you will eventually limit your success.

When we got into real estate, sure we wanted fancy cars and nice watches. If you are into luxury items, reward yourself along the way. However, our WHY is a lifetime pursuit that starts with family. Paying off our parents' mortgage, giving our children everything they could ever dream of, and being able to support the loved ones that sacrificed everything in pursuit of a better life for us. Those are real whys that don't end once you achieve materialistic levels of success.

Why do you want to be successful? Maybe your why isn't your family; maybe it's freedom or faith-related. Remove your ego from the situation and ask yourself, why is it that I really want to be successful? The best way to dig deeper into your why is to ask "and then" questions...

"I want to make a lot of money to get out of my debts."

And then?

"I want to be able to support my mom, so she doesn't have to work."

And then?

"I want to build a team so that I can spend more time with my family."

And then?

"I want to build the biggest company in the world and provide for my children, so they have everything I didn't have growing up."

And then?

"I want to be able to retire early, so I never miss a game and can spend time with my children while my business grows."

In the beginning, the goal was to get out of debt. Your why developed into your mother, your children, and their future. When times get tough, you won't think about your debt, you will think about your mother and your children. That why is so much stronger than making a lot of money and getting out of debt.

## Taking massive action

Once you make your decision to succeed, reprogram your surroundings, and understand your big WHY, it's time to take massive action. If your goals are big and your WHY is significant, then you should expect the work to be difficult. If your goal was to simply get out of debt, you can find hundreds of stable sales jobs that will help you get out of debt.

Your goals became to create generational wealth while taking care of your mother and children. You can't expect to take care of three generations of family members without massive efforts.

Become laser-focused on your goals and spend every minute of every day on reaching them. This won't happen on day one, day seven or day thirty. However, massive action compounded over time will get you results and momentum that perpetuates into reaching those goals. Once you do start seeing the fruits of your labor, delay gratification as long as you can. Continue to invest back into your business and, most importantly, invest in yourself.

The only way to create generational results is by taking massive action and becoming laser-focused on your goals, while always keeping your big WHY in mind.

## Execution

Become obsessed with results, not just action. Massive action is lost without systems and execution. Someone could take massive action trying to hammer a nail into a board with their bare hand. They could work tirelessly, hitting their hand on the nail over and over again. However, someone with a hammer or a nail gun will come along and outperform them. Massive action works best when you equip yourself with the right tools and systems to get the job done. Remember, you are no longer an employee. You are not trying to "look" busy or feel productive because that won't help you retire early and take care of your children. You have now entered a results only mindset, where the only thing that matters is the results you can achieve.

Invest in mentorship and develop your skills, along with daily success habits. Put scalable systems in place when you have a business of one so that you can train your future team when you become a business of ten. Delay gratification invest in your systems and learn them as if you were going to teach them to your first employee.

Once you find your proverbial hammer, then your massive action isn't wasted by appearing busy. Your massive action is pushing you one step closer towards your big WHY each day.

The process and strategy of landing your first deal aren't complicated. Throughout the rest of the book, we will give you our step by step process, along with our scripts. The difficult part is between the ears because you will be tested mentally along the way. Making a decision, committing to that decision, sacrificing short term pleasure for long-term financial freedom, understanding your big WHY, and becoming a master of your craft will help you battle through those difficult times.

There will be times you want to quit. You will get frustrated, exhausted and tested every day. Real estate is simple but not easy, and that should excite you because wealth and financial freedom live on the other side of pain and discomfort. When you feel like quitting, dig deep and just understand that every hurdle along the way is bringing you one step closer to your dreams. Remember, you can have growth or comfort, but you can't have both.

Prepare yourself for the greatest journey of your life, reach out to us at allinnation.com and welcome to ALL-IN Nation.

## CHAPTER 3

# Landing Your First Deal Will Change Your Life Forever

Now that you have made the decision to succeed, it's time to get to work. When we started in real estate over five years ago, there was no blueprint, there were no scripts, and there certainly weren't foolproof, tried, and true strategies that work. The strategies laid out over these next few chapters have helped hundreds of real estate entrepreneurs land their first deal and many more after that. We would advise you not to re-invent the wheel. You will be tempted to take some of these strategies and add your own "twist," but force yourself to stick to these systems, along with the scripts.

Remember, you are here to get wealthy, not rich. Even if you are talented enough to pave your own way and deviate from the script, your first employee might not be. The systems and strategies laid out in this book are replicable. You can teach someone how to read these scripts, and they can teach the next person. So many great entrepreneurs have failed along the way because it's not how much you know, it's what you can teach and train others to do. You don't want to become the plumber who is still driving the truck at 70 years old. You want to become wealthy by creating financial freedom, and more importantly, time freedom.

Our goal with these systems is to give you the systems and scripts that have helped us scale a multi-million-dollar operation. Once you master these skills for yourself, you can use the same system to teach your first employee. It's not what you know; it's what you can teach.

## Explaining wholesaling and legalities

One of the first questions we get from newbies entering the wholesaling industry is, "Is this legal?" Hopefully, by now, you have seen multiple people creating financial freedom through wholesaling. You are probably here because you have seen our success or someone else's success in the industry. Wholesaling is 100% legal, but you do want to make sure you follow the laws and regulations of your particular state.

Each state has its own set of real estate laws and regulations to protect the individuals in the industry. As long as you are not misrepresenting yourself as an agent or the end buyer when you are speaking to sellers, you will not have any issues. What do we mean by that? If you intend on wholesaling real estate, the agreement should state your intent to assign the deal to a third party if you intend to do so. It is also vital to include all contingency clauses as well that will protect yourself and all of the parties involved.

It's also important to know that you do NOT need a license to wholesale real estate, but you should never act as if you are a licensed agent if you are not.

We don't want to overwhelm you with legal jargon, as we are not lawyers and do not provide legal advice. Make sure to check the particular laws in your state to make sure you are in compliance. Do the right thing, don't pretend to be anything you are not, always be honest and you won't have any issues.

If you are worried about contract verbiage or documents you may need, we have you covered. Visit our website at allinnation.com, and we will send you our exact purchase agreements, so you know you are protected.

## The Wholesaling Process

Wholesaling is a process, just like any sales or transaction flow. It starts with you and ends when you cash your first check. As we mentioned, the process is simple, but the work can be difficult. Here is the roadmap that takes you from finding a deal to getting paid:

## Marketing

You can't catch a fish unless you put a hook in the water, and you can't find your first deal unless people know you buy real estate. There are many free and paid marketing channels that range from free to our digital campaigns that cost us over tens of thousands of dollars per month. If people don't know about you, they can't sell you their home. Marketing is vital for your business to grow, and we will discuss every available marketing channel you can use to land your first deal. Think of marketing as an investment and not an expense.

**What is a Motivated Seller?**

The goal of your marketing is to find motivated sellers that are interested in selling their home for a cash offer. What is a motivated seller? A motivated seller is someone who needs to sell their home quickly. Typically, there is a financial, time, or circumstance out of their control that would motivate them to accept a lesser cash offer instead of a traditional listing that can take months to sell. A motivated seller could come as a necessity after a divorce, an unexpected death in the family, an urgent job relocation or any life occurrence that may require a simple and quick transaction.

A motivated seller could also be someone behind on their mortgage, facing foreclosure or in probate. If someone enters foreclosure, they risk losing their home for nothing. A homeowner could also be facing home repairs that they cannot afford. For example, let's say someone needs a full roof repair, and they don't have $15,000 to fix their roof. They can allow their home to become condemned via water damage eventually, or they could walk away with a fair cash offer and move on with their lives.

Disgruntled landlords can also be motivated sellers. Maybe they are having trouble with a property or a tenant that they cannot remove from the property. Selling the property allows them to move on with their lives and may lead to you finding a great deal.

Remember, you are a real estate entrepreneur, not an investor. The reason you get paid will be solely based on your ability to solve problems. None of these deals will get done unless you can create a winning solution for every party involved, and if they accept your offer, that means you solved their problem as best possible. Not every situation will be comfortable because often these sellers are going through difficult times in their lives. Your job is to become a great listener and a solution-oriented partner to help them in their time of need.

Many of the situations listed above are major life issues that cause stress and emotional trauma. If you can offer that solution, you become an invaluable problem solver. Keep that in mind at all times during your conversations with sellers.

**Purchase agreement: Getting the property "under contract"**

Once you can find the solution to your motivated sellers' needs, and you agree on a fair price for the home in its current condition, it's time to sign the contract and finalize the offer. The price will always take into consideration the needed repairs and costs associated with taking on the risks of the property. We will dig into this more later. Once the agreement is in place, it's time to take it to the title agency and begin the escrow process. Remember, if you need a copy of the purchase agreement, check out allinnation.com

## Open escrow

For a transaction to become legal, you must open escrow via an earnest money deposit. That deposit can be as little as $1, and we will discuss later on how to do this the right way and how to find a title agency that is investor-friendly.

## Assigning the contract to a cash buyer

To complete the deal, you will need a cash buyer that will cover the total cost of the agreement. The cash buyer fulfills their end of the deal, and everyone gets paid at the same time (you and the seller). Remember, you are selling the contract to purchase the home, you never actually own the home.

You get paid!

This is the simple process of finding a deal and getting paid. The first time through, it may be a little uncomfortable, and thrilling. The more you go through this process, the more comfortable and confident you will become.

**How does everyone win?**

Does all of this sound too good to be true? How is it possible for everyone to win in this situation? Why would the end buyer be comfortable paying you a commission? How does all of this work?

Remember, the only way deals happen is if everyone benefits and never underestimate the value you hold in each transaction. When you find a motivated seller and help them out of their current situation, you also acquire the contract to a very valuable asset, the right to purchase a property that wouldn't be available otherwise. These properties are not available on the MLS or traditional marketplaces typically, which means you are holding an asset that real estate investors need in order to make money. Real estate investors don't make money unless they have inventory. Let's go through an example:

You find a motivated seller that needs to be out of their home in the next 30 days. You do your research and find that when the home is in mint condition, it is worth $300,000. The problem for the seller is that the home needs a new roof, and there are foundation issues, making it impossible to list the home with a traditional agent. After using our repair calculator, you estimate the home needs $35,000 in repairs to sell for top dollar. After doing the math and understanding the situation, you offer the seller $175,000 as a cash offer.

The seller is pleased because they just covered the balance of their mortgage and walked away with additional proceeds. If the condition of the home got worse, they could risk the property being condemned and potentially losing the property for nothing. You then assign the contract to the real estate investor for $195,000. The investor is happy because they know that after completing the repairs for $35,000, they can then sell the home for $300,000.

The seller receives $175,000

You receive $20,000

The real estate investor makes $49,000 after fixing the home

**ARV (Actual Retail Value):** $300,000

**Agreement Price:** $175,000

**Investor Price:** $195,000

**Agency Fees/Closing Costs:** $21,000 (7%)

**Investor Repairs:** $35,000

**Investor Profit:** $49,000

**Your Profit:** $20,000

Get our exact ARV calculator at allinnation.com.

This situation occurs thousands of times every single day across the U.S., and it's your job to find more of these situations. You make your $20,000 without ever risking any of your own money, and you are free to find the next deal.

But what happens if you put the home under contract and then you can't find a buyer?

If you are using our cost estimator tools, getting accurate ARV (After Repair Value) numbers, and building a solid buyer list, you should never run into this problem. However, there are times when something unforeseen happens, and the deal isn't what you expected. In our contract, there is a clause that states "subject to financial partners approval or inspection period."

While you don't want to use that clause unless there is no other alternative, this protects you and removes the risk of the situation. Without that clause, you would be left liable for purchasing the property.

Now, let's go through all of the ways you can market yourself and your business to find more of these deals and start cashing checks.

## CHAPTER 4

# Free Marketing Channels

Marketing yourself and your business is the only way to find these motivated sellers. If you are like we were, you might be starting from zero. When we started in real estate, we didn't have big budgets, but we did have a strong WHY and an unrelenting work ethic. No marketing is truly free because, as you will find out, your time is your most valuable asset. However, if you don't have a marketing budget, your sweat equity is your marketing budget.

## Driving for dollars

As long as you have a vehicle, the best place you can start is driving for dollars. Why is it called that? Because you can literally make hundreds of thousands of dollars driving around "hot" areas and searching for vacant or distressed properties.

Where should you go and what should you look for?

Distressed properties are exactly as they sound, they need work and a lot of it. If you need a place to start, search the MLS or Zillow to find locations where a lot of recent properties have been sold. These are your hot areas. Once you find a general area, start driving the streets looking for vacant properties or properties that need a lot of work.

The best indicators of a distressed property include:

- Boarded up doors or windows
- High grass (lack of maintenance)
- Foreclosure/notice signs on the doors
- Damaged roof or windows
- Extreme/unlivable wear and tear

Once you find a distressed property, write down the address and keep a great log of each property you see. After you build up a list of at least 100 of these properties, you will need to go to your local county assessor to find the owners information.

After you find your list and get the owner information from the country assessor, you will need to find the owners contact information. The owner doesn't live there, so the only way to find that information is by skip tracing the information you receive from the county assessor.

## What is skip tracing?

Skip tracing is the process of locating someone's whereabouts and contact information.

You can skip trace these leads for around .15 to .35 cents per contact if you are starting with a small list. Make sure you are using a reliable company because the cost of getting the wrong information could make the difference between a deal that could make you ten or $20,000. Our recommendation is needtoskip.com or visit allinnation.com for other resources.

Driving for dollars can be very lucrative because it costs less than $100 between gas and skip tracing.

Once you find their contact information, there are a few ways you can contact the owner.

## Door Knocking

Door knocking is as self-explanatory as it sounds. Once you have the owners information, you can either visit them or write them a letter (next section). Knocking on their door can be a little intimidating at first, but if you approach it the right way, with confidence and a polite tone, it is the best way to get in front of the homeowner.

Start by introducing yourself and let them know you are a real estate investor. Kindly let them know that you are working on some other projects in the area and ask if they would be interested in selling their property at (address). Again, you may get some pushback, and you might get a few doors slammed in your face, but that no is moving you one step closer to your first deal.

## Door knock the properties in hot areas

If you find a hot area and manage to find a few distressed properties, take advantage of every opportunity you can by introducing yourself to the neighbors in the area. Real estate is a numbers game and the more people you speak to, the closer you will get to your first deal. Knock on the neighbors' door and say:

"Hello, my name is ____

I am a real estate investor in the area. I wanted to introduce myself because I have a project going on a few blocks from here. If you or anybody you know wants to sell their property for cash, please reach out to me (hand them your business card). I also pay a $500 referral fee for anyone you connect me with if we are able to buy their home."

Keep it simple and keep it friendly. The homeowner you door knock may be a motivated seller or know somebody in the area that wants to sell their home. Every conversation could be your first deal, and you should always keep that in mind.

## Send handwritten letters

If you don't feel comfortable knocking on the homeowners' door, you need to get over that fear quickly because talking to people is the name of the game. However, if you feel more comfortable writing them a letter, you can do that as well. The letter should look like this:

"Hello _______

My name is _____, and I'm interested in purchasing your house at (Address).

I am a local home buyer, and I can buy your house in "As-Is" condition and pay cash. You don't have to worry about repairs, commissions, or closing costs. I can purchase it fast and will keep it hassle-free.

Please contact me anytime at (**Phone Number**) if you would like to discuss selling your house at a fair price.

Sincerely,

(your name)—Phone #

Visit (website name) for your offer.

Note: You want to keep your calls organized, and as you get further into other marketing channels, it's best to use a trackable phone # that isn't your personal number. Consider getting a Google phone # to start.

**Cold calling**

Becoming a great cold caller is the number one asset to your business or any business. If we could recommend one skill that will make you millions of dollars in this industry, it's cold calling. If you can learn to get comfortable and confident on the phone, speaking with sellers, the sky is the limit for your business. Once you have your list of properties, you can call each person on the list and attempt to speak with them directly over the phone and either negotiate a price over the phone (not recommended if you are new) or set up a time to meet them at the property.

Cold calling is both a free and paid strategy because as your business grows, you will end up investing a lot of your marketing dollars into purchasing lists and skip tracing those lists before making your calls. However, the phone calls are free, and cold calling is one of the most significant assets we use in our businesses. We have spent years mastering the art of the perfect script, and as a gift to you for purchasing this book, we wanted to include our exact cold calling script in this book.

Remember to stick to the script! No matter how tempted you are to deviate from the script, STICK TO IT. The script will save you time, ensure you get the information you need and create a structure you can teach once you begin to scale.

## Outbound Calling Script

ME: Hi is this (Name)

**Client: Yes, this is him how can I help you?**

ME: Yes, my name is (Your Name) and I'm calling in regards to your property located at (Property Address).

**Client: Okay, what about it?**

ME: Great, the reason I'm calling is because I work with a local investor in the area and we are looking to purchase 1 more house in your neighborhood. We can make you a cash offer today if you are interested in selling? We'd love to potentially buy it if we are a good fit.

**THEM: Yes, what's your offer?**

Me: Great! Well, we don't run Evaluations until we get interest on your side, but let me give you some information regarding what we do and our process. We are not Realtors, but Home Buyers. That means there are no commissions involved. We also buy your property by paying cash in AS IS condition which means you don't have to make any repairs and we will also take care of your closing costs. Sounds good??

**Them: Yes.**

ME: Great, our process is very simple, first, we'll get some information about your property, mainly the condition it's in and any updates you've made. And then we have our Acquisitions Manager call you back with our Evaluation on your home, how does that sound?

**THEM: YES**

Me: Great, can you tell me a little bit about the property? (Insert into Podio webform)

1. If you don't mind me asking is there any particular reason for selling?
2. How's the condition inside? Any major upgrades?
3. Do you have tenants or are you occupying the property?

Me: Great, I have all the information I need. I'll go ahead and have my manager run the numbers and he will call you back within 24-48 hours with a CASH offer. I appreciate your time, thank you and have a great day.

**END of script**—Get these exact scripts and more at allinnation.com

In a perfect world, every call will go smoothly, and our leads will be excited to speak with us when we call. We don't live in a perfect world, and almost no call will go exactly as scripted. You will run into people that are angry that you called, people will hang up on you, or they won't let you finish your sentences. Cold calling isn't pretty sometimes, but every time you do face adversity, you are moving one step closer to your yes. Remember, your perseverance will be what makes you fortunes in the long run.

After spending years on the phones and listening to our team make cold calls every day, we have heard just about everything. There are a few common objections that you will hear from potential sellers once you start cold calling. These objections should not be mistaken as them saying, "No." These people don't know you, and they certainly don't know what you can do for them. If you allow a single objection to deter you from continuing the conversation, you are not only hurting yourself, but you are also hurting them. Your job is to communicate what your value is and see if you can help.

Here is a list of common objections you will hear, and the rebuttals you should respond with. Once you overcome each objection, jump right back into the script wherever you left off and continue the conversation.

**Cold Call Rebuttals**

**Where'd you get my number?**

**Best answer:** ** More than likely our marketing department got it from public records. However, were you interested in an offer for your property?

**What's your offer?**

**Best Answer:** To be honest, I don't run the numbers on homes. My manager does. However, If you are interested in selling your home, I can have him give you a call back with an offer.

**What's your company's name/who are you guys?**

**Best Answer:** Our company name is (business name). We are local home buyers in the neighborhood that buy, sell and rent here in the (location) area.

**Where are you guys located?**

**Best answer:** We are located in the (location) area, our office is in (enter location).

**I haven't really been thinking about it.**

**Best answer:** Well, would you be curious in a callback with a cash offer?

**"Your offer is going to be too low so I am not interested"**

**Best answer:** I can respect that, I just want to mention our offer is typically up there with the highest of them and we are serious cash buyers.

**So how does your company or process work?**

**Best answer:** Very simple, if you're interested in selling or taking a cash offer I just have a few questions for you and my boss will call you back within 24-48 hours with our offer.

**"Just make me an offer"**

**Best answer:** Okay sure thing, what's the condition of the property, how many bedrooms..etc.? (GO STRAIGHT INTO PROPERTY QUESTIONS) and when finished asking questions just wrap up the call and say "My boss will be calling you back tomorrow with our offer"

## Cold Calling Tips

If you are new to sales or new to real estate, cold calling can be intimidating. We have seen more aspiring real estate entrepreneurs fail at this business because of call reluctance. Real estate is a numbers game, and you should expect a majority of the people you call, won't want to talk to you. Don't take it personally because they don't know you and they certainly don't know how you can help them. The truth is, people will hang up on you, and some may even get angry because you called. If you don't set an appointment, then you won't ever see or hear from the person again, so what's the worst that could happen?

If you can push beyond the fear of picking up the phone and making the calls, you are already ahead of most aspiring entrepreneurs. Your goal for each call should be to get through the script and get as many answers to those questions as possible. If you don't finish the script, you are doing yourself an injustice, and most importantly, you are doing the seller an injustice because you may have a solution for a problem they didn't know they had.

Every phone call is an opportunity, and it's your job to educate each person on how you can help. Even if you can't help them, they may know somebody that needs your help. All you can do is find out if they are interested in selling their house. Once you put your ego aside and get over the fear of rejection, what do you have to lose? Nothing. What do you have to gain? Everything.

### Other free marketing resources

If you are starting from zero, your word of mouth and sweat equity is your biggest asset. Start with every free resource available to you, including for sale by owner websites. Marketplace sites like Craigslist, Zillow FSBO (for sale by owner), and FSBO.com are great places to start. You may be faced with a lot of competition, because free will attract the masses, but if you are persistent and can get your foot in the door first, you might be able to land your first deal through these resources.

Make sure to check daily because new listings and properties are always being added. If a listing sits there for 48 hours before you call them, chances are, they have already received dozens of calls from hungry investors looking for a deal. Real estate is a competitive industry, and while first doesn't always win, it increases your chances.

### Local real estate groups

Your goal as a real estate entrepreneur is to tell everyone you can about who you are and what you do. Local REIA's (Real

Estate Investor Associations) sound like a place to find competition, not deals. However, you will come to find out that most real estate investors want to help you on your path to success. There are more than enough deals to be had, even in the most crowded marketplaces. Local REIA's are a great place to meet likeminded individuals and learn more about your craft. You might not find deals here, but you can find real estate investors (that will buy your deals), information about hot areas, sales tips/tricks, or mentorship from people that have walked in your shoes. Remember what we said about associating yourself with the right people? REIA's are a great place to start.

### Facebook groups/marketplaces

Local Facebook groups are another great place to search for deals if you don't have a marketing budget. Sure, you can find investor groups that are similar to REIA's, but you can also create a flyer sharing what you do, along with your company phone number. Be sure to include that you buy houses; you buy AS-IS, you pay all CASH, and can close quickly. This verbiage will resonate with a motivated seller, and you are likely to receive calls if you do this enough, consistently. Look for local groups that include phrases like yard sale, FSBO (for sale by owner), flea market or other local marketplaces in your area.

### Flyers/business cards

If you have a small budget of a few hundred dollars, the first thing you should invest in is business cards or flyers. None of these marketing strategies are truly free, and even driving for dollars will cost money in gas. Find a way to make a few hundred dollars to invest in business cards or flyers that you can distribute while door knocking or meeting people. Another idea is to leave business cards on car windows in hot areas. Make sure your flyer or business card tells people that you pay a referral fee if they refer someone to you, and you purchase their home. If somebody doesn't know you, the best motivator in the world is money.

### Referrals

Word of mouth marketing! We can't preach this enough; every person you know should know that you are a real estate investor. If you are worried that they will laugh or respond with a snarky comment, use it as fuel. At least now they know what you do, and after you land a few deals, they will be asking you for a job. Start by writing down 100 people you know and call them one by one, letting them know what you do.

Sure, it might be uncomfortable sharing your new venture, but you are learning to get comfortable being uncomfortable. When we started in real estate, our family and friends didn't always believe in us either. Don't let that slow your progress or your confidence. Your future results will speak for themselves, and you will find out that many of those people will be your biggest cheerleaders along your journey to success.

Getting your first deal is difficult because you are starting from zero. A good friend of ours likes to say, a rocket takes 62 miles to reach outer space, and the first mile is the toughest. Anytime you start something new, it will take some time to build momentum, but once you do, things start to get easier. Don't be afraid to get your hands dirty, look at every opportunity, and fight every day to get your first deal. For some, it may take a few months, but once you land your first 5-figure check, it will all be worth it. Once you land your first deal, you can invest back into the paid marketing channels that will build your business.

If you have any questions about how to take advantage of these free marketing channels, reach out to us directly at allinnation.com.

# CHAPTER 5

# Paid Marketing Channels

If you are reading this book, you are probably either just starting your real estate journey, or you have landed a few deals and are looking to take your business to the next level. If you are like us, you are likely starting with a small or minimal budget. If that describes you, then spend every second investing in yourself and your craft, while working towards landing your first deal. Work on your cold calling script, get comfortable speaking to sellers, knock on doors, and tell everyone what you do.

While you are doing that, find a way to make at least a few hundred dollars to invest in flyers, business cards, and an initial set of leads you can cold call to perfect your skills. You can read every book in the world, but there is no substitution for getting your hands dirty and doing the work.

Your goal should be to perfect your craft and become so skilled, that paid marketing becomes a vehicle to grow your business and not a wasted budget. So many newbies in real estate have a few thousand dollars to invest, and they are excited to jump-start their business, but they haven't taken the time to perfect their skills. You could buy the best golf clubs and golf equipment in the world, but if you haven't spent time on the driving range hitting thousands of golf balls, none of that equipment matters.

Think no differently about your craft in real estate. You need repetition and an intense focus on perfecting your skills, along with your systems. Otherwise, you will waste thousands of dollars expanding when your skills are not ready. Remember the phrase; success is when preparation meets opportunity. If you have spent thousands of hours making cold calls, knocking on doors and talking to sellers, you will be ready to expand once you have the marketing dollars to invest.

Once you do land your first deal, you will be tempted to feed your ego to prove all of your doubters wrong. It's tempting to run out and buy a new car or a watch to show everyone that you were right, but you didn't start down this path to land one deal and look rich. You started because you wanted to become wealthy, and wealth requires patience, along with delayed gratification. You can't rush any part of the growth process, and your goal is to invest everything you have back into the business. Every second, every dollar and every ounce of energy you can invest back into your business will return itself 10X over if you can delay gratification for your future self.

We spent our first two years investing every dollar back into our business by perfecting our skills and spending every dollar we earned on marketing. That investment allowed us to scale both our marketing budgets and our team to help us expand our operation. That investment will enable you to build wealth, both in time and financial freedom. Over that time, we have watched countless aspiring entrepreneurs land their first deal and indulge in ego-based purchases. People immediately forget how hard it was to land that first deal, and instead of saving to invest back into their business, they purchase a car. The next month they are complaining because they have no money to invest into marketing and the month after that, they are broke again.

Instead, think about your business at scale. What could your business have been if you put that $15,000 into marketing and turned it into $150,000? Once you start to scale your business and put systems in place, you will begin to value the potential of your money. You will begin to understand how every dollar invested becomes amplified, and once that process is perfected, your money begins to multiply exponentially. That is how you build real wealth instead of simply looking rich. That is true financial freedom!

You will find that many of the skills and practices you used in the free marketing channels will serve you well when it becomes time to invest in paid marketing channels. You practiced your calls, writing letters, talking to sellers, making offers, and presenting prices so much that you can't mess it up. Now, your marketing dollars turn into more profits instead of wasted leads.

## Data = Foundation

Great data is the foundation of any marketing campaign. Why? Because inaccurate data wastes time and money. You will spend thousands targeting the wrong people and not having success. More importantly, there is an opportunity cost because your competition will have a massive advantage if they have more accurate data.

## Pulling lists

Before you can invest in any paid marketing strategies, it's essential that you have a list to target.

How do you know who might be a motivated seller?

It's impossible to know for sure, but there is a predictive criterion that helps narrow down our search. Typically, a motivated seller will be a home with high equity and the last sale date of 20+ years old. These targets mean the home has been owned for a while. It also means that the mortgage is either paid off or close to being paid off. The home could require major repairs if not properly kept, and the home has the equity paid into it, that might make sense to consider a cash offer.

You can start your lead search at listsource.com and use the following criteria:

**1.High Equity Absentee List**

- 30+ % equity
- Choose a city or a few zip codes (important to know your hot areas)
- Property type: SFR (Single Family Residence)
- Last market sale date (Before 12/31/1999)

**2.High Equity Owner Occupied List**

- 50+% equity
- Choose a city or a few zip codes
- Property type: SFR (Single Family Residence)
- Last market sale date (Before 12/31/1999)

**Other lists include:**

- Pre-foreclosure

- Tax Defaults/ Delinquent
- 20+ year ownership
- Seniors (55+ at least 20%+ equity)
- No data list

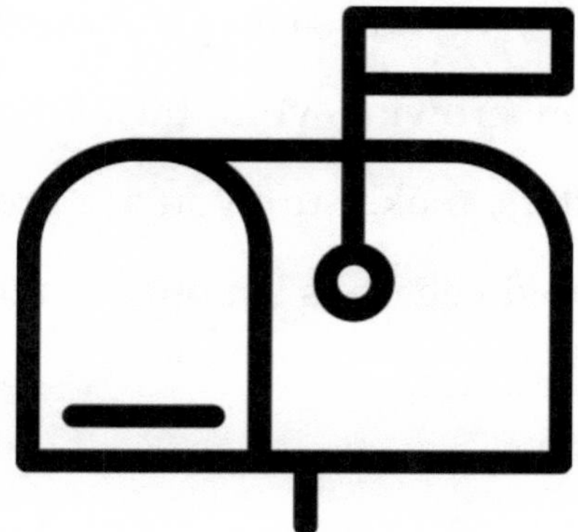

**Direct mail**

Remember the letter you wrote to the seller you found while door knocking? Think about writing that letter to thousands of people instead of just a few. Direct mail is one of the most predictable, tried, and true marketing strategies in real estate. Why? Because real estate is a numbers game and if enough people see your offer, you will find people that need your help. If you are starting with a small budget, you will need to write these letters by hand, which will take hours. That's how we started as well, but once you do have a budget, there are services that will write those letters for you.

Consider using a service like Turboletters.com that will write these handwritten quality yellow letters for you. Each letter costs as little as .50 cents and saves you hours of your time that you can focus on growing your business. Once you start mailing these letters, make sure you are prepared to answer calls because you will get calls if a seller is motivated to sell or to inquire about an offer.

**Bandit signs**

You have probably seen the "We Buy Houses" signs around your town. Almost every successful real estate entrepreneur utilizes these signs because they get a response and are very affordable. When we started in real estate, we didn't have the money to purchase pre-printed signs, so we would spend hours handwriting "We Buy Houses" and our phone number via a bold Sharpie marker. Blank signs start at around .70 cents per sign.

We recommend investing just a little more and buying pre-printed signs for around $1.50 per sign. These signs are easier to read if a motivated seller is driving by the area and makes you look more professional in the process.

Bandit signs are highly effective ways to market your services, but they are called bandit signs for a reason. The city doesn't approve of putting these signs out, and if they see them, city workers will remove them. These signs are not in compliance with city code, so if you want to get the most visibility from them, you need to put them out when city workers are not there to remove them.

We recommend putting signs out on Friday night, after the city workers have gone home for the weekend. Most investors don't worry about losing signs after that, but if you are concerned about losing your signs, you may want to pick them up on Sunday night. We recommend leaving them there. Sure, some of your signs might get picked up by city workers. However, some signs may stay up for weeks or even months if placed in the proper location (or with a bit of luck). A well-placed sign could result in multiple calls and potentially tens of thousands of dollars in your pocket.

Where should you place these signs?

Similar to billboards, traffic is key. The more people that see your signs equals more potential phone calls. Start with busy intersections in and around your hot areas. These are the areas most likely to have motivated sellers, and if someone is motivated, they are more likely to call. Bandit signs receive highly motivated seller calls, and there is a reason these signs are so popular.

### Cold calling

Cold calling is both a free and paid marketing channel because it can cost as little as the price of 100 skip traced leads, or as much as the tens of thousands we spend on lists monthly. We spend massive budgets each month pulling and skip tracing lists because cold calling is the best way to locate motivated sellers (if you are good on the phones). This is why we stress the importance of perfecting your craft before making large marketing investments. You could be the hardest worker in the world, but if you haven't perfected your ability to talk to sellers, move through your script, overcome objections, and present offers, you are wasting time, as well as money.

Once you or your team become great at cold calling, the cost is just sweat equity and allows you to connect with motivated sellers right away. If you are wondering how it's possible to make thousands of calls each day, there is a smarter way. Investing in a dialer will save you hours spent dialing and reaching voicemails. Allindialer.com is a great resource to get your own call dialer. The dialer makes calls for you and only connects you once someone answers the phone. This allows you to spend your time speaking with people instead of making phone calls.

Again, make sure you are investing in sales mentorship or have a coach that can help you perfect your cold calling and closing skills. Once you do have the budgets to invest, you may decide that you don't want to spend hours making phone calls each day. If that's you, consider hiring a team of closers that will make calls and generate leads for you. Callgeeks.com takes all of the guesswork out of your cold calling and allows you to spend more time closing deals. Don't forget the importance of skip tracing as well, because the only way to connect with the right seller is to make sure you have accurate contact information.

If you are cold calling, make sure to seek legal counseling to ensure you are in TCPA compliance. For more cold calling tips go to allinnation.com.

**Outbound Calling Script**

ME: Hi is this (Name)

**Client: Yes, this is him how can I help you?**

ME: Yes, my name is (Your Name) and I'm calling in regards to your property located at (Property Address).

**Client: Okay, what about it?**

ME: Great, the reason I'm calling is because I work with a local investor in the area and we are looking to purchase 1 more house in your neighborhood. We can make you a cash offer today if you are interested in selling? We'd love to potentially buy it if we are a good fit.

**THEM: Yes, what's your offer?**

Me: Great! Well, we don't run Evaluations until we get interest on your side, but let me give you some information regarding what we do and our process. We are not Realtors, but Home Buyers. That means there are no commissions involved. We also buy your property by paying cash in AS IS condition which means you don't have to make any repairs and we will also take care of your closing costs. Sounds good??

**Them: Yes.**

ME: Great, our process is very simple, first, we'll get some information about your property, mainly the condition it's in and any updates you've made. And then we have our Acquisitions Manager call you back with our Evaluation on your home, how does that sound?

**THEM: YES**

Me: Great, can you tell me a little bit about the property? (Insert into Podio webform)

1. If you don't mind me asking is there any particular reason for selling?

2. How's the condition inside? Any major upgrades?

3. Do you have tenants or are you occupying the property?

Me: Great, I have all the information I need. I'll go ahead and have my manager run the numbers and he will call you back within 24-48 hours with a CASH offer. I appreciate your time, thank you and have a great day.

**END of script--** Get these exact scripts and more at allinnation.com

## PPC/Google ads

If you want to separate yourself from your competitors, you have to market where they are not. Direct mail, cold calling, door knocking, and bandit signs have been staple marketing practices for years. They are the lowest cost entry point into real estate investing, so everyone starts there. As you keep expanding, you will realize that you need to become omnipresent with your marketing. Your goal is to find motivated sellers in every place they could be searching.

People today start many of their searches online and only trust what they find on Google. It's vital that you create a web presence via your website and social media. Your website and your social media presence build trust with potential sellers, which gives you the best chance of getting their phone call.

If you have $3000-$10,000 of monthly budget to invest, PPC Google ads generate higher quality leads than any other form of advertising. Why? Because they will find you when searching for terms like "sell my house fast" or "buy my house fast" along with other relevant search terms. Make sure that you use a reputable company that specializes in motivated seller/real estate campaigns. The wrong campaign targeting could result in the wrong type of leads and thousands of dollars wasted. If you are looking for a company that specializes in real estate/investor campaigns, check out our recommendations at allinnation.com.

## SMS/text marketing

Text message open rates are higher than any other channel. SMS marketing has more than a 90% open rate, which means you will actually reach potential motivated sellers right at their fingertips. If you send a letter, most of them get thrown in the trash. If you are cold calling, many people won't answer their phone. Everyone reads their text messages, and SMS marketing yields a 15-20% response rate.

The high response rate is both good and bad because you will undoubtedly receive some angry responses along the way. The goal of your marketing is to receive a response, whether positive or negative. Countless times in our business, we have received angry phone calls that turned into deals after speaking with them. Remember, they can't sell you their home if they don't know about you, and any response could lead to your next deal.

SMS marketing is also very affordable at around .03 cents per delivery. If you are considering SMS marketing, make sure to seek legal counseling to ensure you are in TCPA compliance. For more information and recommendations, check out allinnation.com.

## RVM marketing

Have you ever looked at your notifications and noticed a voicemail, but you never received a phone call? That is called a ringless voicemail, and similar to SMS marketing, it is one of the best ways to generate a response for the same .03 cents per delivery. RVM is a more personable approach because potential sellers can hear your personalized message about who you are and what you do. Again, you are guaranteed to receive some angry calls back from people, and your response to those incoming calls will make the difference in landing deals or not. Your most experienced closer (yourself at first) should be available to receive all PPC, SMS, and RVM phone calls because these are likely to be the most motivated seller leads that come through.

Again, make sure to seek legal counsel to maintain TCPA compliance with all of these campaigns. If you have questions about running RVM campaigns, visit us at allinnation.com.

### Building your buyers list

While you are searching for deals, you want to start building your buyers list. There is nothing worse than putting days of work into landing your first deal, only to lose that deal because you don't have a quality list of buyers to help close the deal. Your buyers will become your partners in this business, and it's essential to build that list before you have a deal to present to them.

The more reputable real estate investors you can add to your list, the better. Why? Real estate investors are savvy, and they are all looking for different criteria when buying deals. You want to have as many options as possible, which will help you make more money while having multiple options to close.

For example, let's say you get a deal under contract for $150,000 in a fixer upper part of town. One investor may be wary of the area and offer $160,000 for the contract, whereas another investor may have just sold a similar home in the area, so they offer $170,000. If you give yourself multiple options, it only increases your chances of finding the right buyer.

How do you build that list?

Real estate investors are typically great at making themselves known if you know where to look. You can start with a site like cashbuyersplus.com where you can find a plethora of cash buyers in your area. All of your meetups and REIA's will pay dividends when searching for cash buyers as well. At most of these local events, you can find several real estate investors or referrals to those buyers. You will find that most people will gladly refer you to their buyers because they are always looking for new deals.

Other resources include Facebook groups, title agency referrals, realtors, or Craigslist. When looking for a buyer, make sure they can close quickly on the deals that you bring them.

## CHAPTER 6

# Walking the Property & Making Offers

Once you make it through the script and get all of the information you need, it's time to walk the property. If you are new to real estate, you never want to make an offer sight unseen. You will notice a lot of real estate entrepreneurs doing "virtual wholesaling," where we buy properties in other markets without looking at them. If you are new to wholesaling, meeting with sellers is vital to your experience and your business. We want you to put in the hours and also know what to look for before you make an offer.

At first, it might be uncomfortable speaking with sellers while thinking about everything you should be looking for when making an offer. Let them know you need to take photos of the property so you can make them a fair offer. It's crucial that you take 30-40 pictures of the entire property so you can estimate just how much money it will take to complete the repairs. Take photos of each room, the corners of the room (for noticeable wear/tear or water damage), carpeting/floors, roof condition, kitchens, bathrooms, and every area of the home that your buyers will want to see.

Taking all of these photos will help you understand what to offer the seller and will also help you qualify your serious buyers to get a ballpark offer before they walk the property.

How do you estimate repair costs?

As you get further into your career, you will learn the costs associated with replacing a roof, kitchen, bathroom, and other key areas. For now, keep your calculations simple with this ARV (After Repair Value) calculator:

**ARV x .70 – Repairs – Wholesale Profit = Your Offer**

Estimated Repair Costs:

Light repairs (new paint/carpet/lighting) $10/Sq. Foot

Mid repairs (New kitchen/bathrooms) $15-20/ Sq. foot

Full rehab (Home in terrible condition) $25+ Sq. foot

For example, you are walking a property that is 2200 square feet has an ARV of $300,000. As you walk the home, you see the kitchen is outdated and that one of the bathrooms will need to be rehabbed. You also know that the carpet and light fixtures will need to be replaced before the home can be sold. The house also needs to be painted to command top dollar on the market. Using our ARV calculator, your offer would look like this:

ARV = $300,000 X.70= $210,000

Mid repairs = $20/sq foot (repairs on the high end)

2200 X $20/sq foot = $44,000 (estimated repairs)

Wholesale profit= $15,000 (at least $10,000 to be worth your time)

$210,000 - $44,000 (repairs) - $15,000 (your profit)= $151,000 offer

Get our exact ARV calculator at allinnation.com.

If in doubt, always start your offer lower than you expect because your seller, and your buyer will try to negotiate with you on both sides. You may have to come up on your price to get the seller to agree, and savvy investors will always try to negotiate your price down if you allow them too. This is why it's so important to help your buyer understand how you came to that price. This is also the reason it's vital to have a strong buyers list. If you have a list of 50 buyers and you price your deals properly, you don't have to worry about buyers negotiating your price down because you have options. If you only have a few buyers on your list, you are left with the best of a few offers instead of 50+.

At this point, we have discussed how to cold call, how to get the information you need before visiting the property, how to determine repairs, and craft your offer. We understand you don't want to flip back and forth through the book when talking to prospects. Our goal was to put together an all in one script, and closers guide so we asked the best two closers in the industry, Andy Garcia and Adrian Salgado to put together an all-in-one closers guide, so you had everything all in one place.

# CHAPTER 7

# All-In Nation Closers Guide

**PITCHING THE PROSPECT**

**SALES SPECIALIST:**

- DIGITAL LEADS: "Hi ______! My name is ______, I'm reaching out regarding some information you filled out on our Website/Facebook.. about selling your property on Main St. You got a minute?"
- COLD CALL LEADS: "Hi ______! My name is ______, I'm reaching out about the conversation you had with one of our agents Yesterday.. He/She mentioned you might be interested in selling the property on Main St. Do you have a minute?"
- RVM LEADS: "Hi ______! My name is ______, Thanks for taking my call, we had previously left you a voicemail/text about selling a property. Are you interested in selling your property?"

- FOLLOW UP LEADS: "Hi ______! My name is ______, I'm reaching out about the conversation we had 1 Week/2 Months/3 Years ago, about buying your property. Everything made sense except: Time/Price/Specific Reason/Etc.. Are you possibly getting any closer to doing anything with the property?"
- FOLLOWED BY SILENCE, WAIT FOR SELLERS RESPONSE.

**Talking Shop**

**SALES SPECIALIST:**

- "Can I ask you a few questions about the property?"

**PROSPECT:**

- "(Something along the lines of, YES, go for it)"..

**SALES SPECIALIST:**

- "Great, I just want to see if there's anything we can do to make an offer. The first thing I need to know. Is your property currently: Rented out, Vacant, are you Living there? What's the situation? "

**PROSPECT:**

- "My property is currently: Rented, Vacant, I live here."

**Questions to ask seller about occupancy**
**SALES SPECIALIST:**
**RENTED:**

- "Are your tenants aware that you are selling?"
- "How have the tenants treated you?"
- "How will your tenants react when they know you sold the property?"
- "Do your tenants have a plan in place for when you sell the property?"

**VACANT:**

- "When is the last time you personally checked on the property?"
- "What was the situation before the property became vacant?"
- "How long has the property been vacant?"

- "If you don't sell the property do you plan on keeping it vacant? What's your next plan with the property?"

**OWNER OCCUPIED:**

- "I want to do my best to provide amazing service, can I ask you. What's your plan after this? Did you and your family have somewhere to get into? Is there anything we can do to help?"
- "As far as time goes, what would be an ideal time frame that you would want all of this done in? Meaning closing & vacate."
- "How long have you lived there?"

**CHECKPOINT**

The Wolf's Closing Guide does NOT go into detail on Building Rapport. Ensure along the way you are constantly Building rapport whenever seller mentions any: Common interests, Likes, Dislikes, Work, Family, Personal Factors that can sidetrack business talk and keep the conversation personal. 80% Rapport Building & 20% Business.

**1st ballpark attempt**

**SALES SPECIALIST:**

- "Can I ask you; I know its early.. BUT did you have any idea where you would need to be at minimum to even be able to consider selling the property?"

**PROSPECT:**

This will go 1 of 2 ways. Seller will either provide you with their ballpark number or you will be shut down.

**SALES SPECIALIST:**

BALLPARK #: "Thank you for providing me with that, I just want to make sure we work around what you're needing out of the property, that's the best way to handle business.. By making sure our Sellers get what they want.. Or at least as close as we can offer to that."

MOVE ON, EVEN IF THEIR BALLPARK NUMBER IS A DEAL.

NO BALLPARK #: "No worries I was just asking because we want to make sure we are even in your ballpark."

DON'T BE UPSET OR AWKWARD THAT NUMBER WASN'T PROVIDED, MAKE PROSPECT FEEL COMFORTABLE, MOVE ON.

**Discussing condition**
**SALES SPECIALIST:**

"I appreciate you providing me all the information I need so far. This just helps me do my job better for YOU. The next thing I need to know is the condition. What's the condition of your property like?"

**PROSPECT:**

- "My property is in Great/Good/Excellent condition"

**SALES SPECIALIST:**

- "When was the last time you did any work to the property?"
- "What type of upgrades have you done to the property?"

**PROSPECT:**

- "Well, to be honest. It's not in great shape and has definitely seen the best of its days. It NEEDS work."

**SALES SPECIALIST:**

- "What are some of the major issues that the property has?"
- "Is doing the remodel an option for you? Sure, it might take more time, energy, & money BUT you could get a bit more."
- "Look, I know you're not a contractor but what would you estimate the rehab cost of this property at?"

**MAKE SELLER CONFIRM THEIR PROPERTY COULD USE THE FOLLOWING:**

- Flooring
- Stainless steel appliances
- Granite & Backsplash
- Cabinets
- Tiled in showers, New Vanity's

- Roofing
- AC Unit
- 'Grey's & White's'
- OR

**PROSPECT:**

- "My property needs ZERO work. It's in great condition, I've done some work in the last few years and kept the property up while I've Lived Here/Rented Property.. It's really in great shape."

**SALES SPECIALIST:**

At this point get Seller engaged if they feel there is no repairs needed to be done to the home

- "When's the last time the floors were replaced?"
- "Does your property have stainless steel appliances?"
- "Does your kitchen have granite countertops & backsplash?"
- "How old are the cabinets?"

- "Does your bathroom have marble tiled in showers, and new vanity's? "
- "When was the last time the roof was replaced?"
- "How old is the AC unit?"
- "As far as the trim goes, does the house have the 'greys and whites'?"

**PROSPECT:**

- "No, my property doesn't have any of those things, it's up to you if you wanted to do that on your own."

**SALES SPECIALIST:**

- "Our plan is to buy the property as is. The largest group of home buyers are currently looking for the Grey's & Whites along with the modern styles. As a result, in our business we are forced to do all these upgrades.. Basically, keeping up with the Jones'"

**FOLLOWED BY:**

- "Now, I do want to make it clear. This is a business and I have to pay my guys and keep the lights on. We're not looking to get rich off your property, but we do have to make a little bit of profit. This doesn't mean you can't sell your home as is and STILL get a fair & competitive price if this is the route you choose to go"

**CHECKPOINT**

By this point, you should have enough insight to know if you should keep it Personable or Professional. Time & Numbers will always win in this game if the prospect is not fully engaged in what you are saying decide if you should go for the kill or continue building massive amounts of rapport.

**Reason for selling**
**SALES SPECIALIST:**

- "Thanks for all the information you've provided me with so far. It's really helping me. If you don't mind me asking , what's the main reason selling has even crossed your mind?"

**PROSPECT:**

- PROVIDED REASON "Okay, so here's what's happening ____________."

**SALES SPECIALIST**

- "(Build a ton of rapport, Make Seller feel like you really care. I cannot script this step; EVERY situation is different.. Be a Friend, Mentor, Listener.)"

**PROSPECT:**

- NO REASON PROVIDED "I really don't see how this applies to the sale of my home. It does not matter, why do you even want to know?"

**SALES SPECIALIST:**

- "The reason I'm asking is because a lot of the time we can help in areas that don't even involve your property, we understand selling a home can be stressful and we just want to make sure we offer our help however we can."

**2nd ballpark attempt**
**SALES SPECIALIST:**

- "What's the balance remaining on the mortgage?"

**PROSPECT:**

- PROVIDED MORTGAGE: "I owe _____ on my mortgage."

**SALES SPECIALIST:**

- "Okay good to know. Now.. Let me ask you, when it's all said and done, and you've sold the house. How much money did you need to have in your pockets once the mortgage is paid off?"

**PROSPECT:**

- NO MORTGAGE: "I don't have a mortgage; I own this property Free & Clear!"

**SALES SPECIALIST:**

- "Good for you, congratulations! That's a good feeling. Let me ask you, when it's all said and done, and you've sold the house. How much money did you need to have in your pockets to even consider selling?"

**PROSPECT:**

- DID NOT DISCLOSE: "It really doesn't matter, I don't see how it applies."…

**SALES SPECIALIST:**

- "I'm asking because we have to make sure any offer we put on the table can cover any loans or mortgages in place, it's just part of the process."

**Final Details**

**SALES SPECIALIST:**

- "Thank you once again. For all the information you have provided me with so far this really helps me. As you might guess, ANY offer comes down to how the property sits. Are there any major damages we should know about? Such as; Water & Fire Damages, Foundation issues or anything crazy? Or really anything else I should know about?"

**PROSPECT:**

- "(Something along the lines of YES, I forgot to mention abc OR NO, we actually got it all covered, I filled you in on everything you need to know)"

**3rd ballpark attempt**
**SALES SPECIALIST:**

- "Mr. Seller, so far I've gotten the impression that you're a smart individual who knows what they want, who is educated… Now, you mean to tell me that YOU have ZERO Idea on what you're looking to get out of this property?"

**PROSPECT:**

- PROVIDED BALLPARK: "Okay, I figured I'd need to be at x amount to even consider selling the property"

**SALES SPECIALIST:**

- "Thank you this helps me out a lot. I'm just doing my job so we can work around your needs. That's the best way to do business, right? By making our customers happy."

**PROSPECT:**

- DOES NOT PROVIDE BALLPARK: "I would really just prefer for YOU to make me an offer, I know what I want but I'm not going to tell you."

**SALES SPECIALIST:**

- "Say no more, I won't ask again. It just helps me do my job better, but I will move on."

## Checkpoint

The time to make an offer is approaching. Your prospect should be fully engaged and comfortable that you are making a legitimate inquiry to purchase their property. ANY & ALL OFFERS PRESENTED MUST BE MADE WITH ABSOLUTE CONFIDENCE.

## Making an offer

**SALES SPECIALIST:**

- 3 Different ways to 'Make an Offer'
- "So far I have a really clear understanding of what the property is and what your situation is. I know it sounds

like you can benefit from some our services. What I can do at this point is: 30 Day closing, I'm buying your property exactly as it sits, I will even pay your closing & title fees... with that said, I would need to be anywhere in the range of 180-200k… Is this something that would interest you?"

- "I'm just sorta doing my homework on this, however I know now at quick glance.. If I was going to make an offer, I can buy your property as-is. I also know based off our conversation the property needs work, so no crazy inspections needed either. I can close in 2-3 weeks… To give you an idea: Ballpark I would need to be in the 180-200k range, and I'll even cover your closing costs. Would that be something that might interest you?"
- "Here's what I can do for you. I know I haven't seen the place but as long as I can confirm all the information you provided me with I know that I can buy your property exactly as it stands, I can close as soon as you're ready.. and on top of that I'll cover ALL closing costs. Ballpark I would be anywhere around the 180-200k range. Is this something you would be interested in?"

For our exact scripts and other resources to help you close more deals, visit allinnation.com.

**Seller Signs Purchase Agreement**

As you can see, there are many possibilities for each conversation. Don't let that overwhelm you because just like anything else, it takes repetition to become an expert. This is why we stress the importance of making cold calls, role-playing conversations with others, and understanding every detail of your pitch. Repetition creates confidence, and confidence is what closes. You could learn every aspect of this script perfectly, but if the seller doesn't feel the confidence in your tone, you will lose them. Likewise, if you miss something from the script, but present your tone as a confident professional, you may still land the deal.

The goal of each part of the conversation is to advance the conversation to the next step. Continue advancing the conversation until eventually presenting your offer with confidence and closing the sale. If you read through that script once, go back and read it again. Then say it aloud over and over again until you know it in your sleep. The great ones practice until they get it right, but the best practice until they can't get it wrong.

Sellers will be able to feel your tone and confidence either in person or over the phone. If they feel as if you are the professional and you can explain your position, along with your offer, you give yourself the best chance to close the deal. There will also be times that you build rapport and go through this process seamlessly, but they still don't accept your offer. Don't let that discourage you. Remember, this is a numbers game, and the fortune is made in the follow-up or on the next call.

## CHAPTER 8

# Closing the Deal

*"You have yourself a deal"*

If you ask us, there are no better words in business. You will never forget your first deal. For some people, it takes a few weeks; for some, it takes months. It took Alex Saenz nine months to close his first deal, and he credits all of his success to battling through those difficult times.

Whenever you do finally close your first deal, none of the difficult times matter, and a euphoric relief will race over you. For many people, their first check is likely the biggest payday of your life. Now it's time to get your buyers together, take the deal to the title company, and get paid. You have done all of the hard work; now it's time to finish the process.

## Finding a title agency

Working with a great title agency will make you a fortune and save you headaches along the way. Not every title company understands wholesaling, though, and the last thing you want is to have a deal fall through at the end because you chose the wrong title agency. Finding an investor-friendly title agency isn't difficult, but it is essential. The right title agency will ensure everything runs smoothly while also saving you money on fees (they will usually give you a 20-30% discount if you find the right title agency).

The best way to find a title agency is by referral. Your networking from Facebook Groups and REIA's should make finding a title agency simple. Getting referred is the best way to find a great partner to help things run smoothly. If you are struggling to find a referral, simply Google "title agencies" and start making phone calls to find an "investor-friendly title agency that works with wholesalers." That verbiage should tell them all they need to know.

## Pre-qualify your buyers

At this point, you know what the house is worth, you know what repair costs are (estimated), and you know the price you need to receive to satisfy your fee. It's time to send pictures and numbers to your buyers' list to see who is interested. Make sure to send the full set of photos so buyers can see the whole picture. There is no point in trying to "trick" buyers into thinking a situation is better than it is. If you attempt to mislead a buyer, they will find out once they view the property, and you risk wasting everyone's time. They should be able to see the photos and your asking price. Make sure to include your fee as well, and feel free to start a little higher than your bottom line. If you have a large buyers list, you can be more selective, but many buyers will try to negotiate down. If you start with a higher number, the worst-case scenario is they accept it, and you make a higher profit.

## Walking buyers through properties

Once you pre-qualify your most interested buyers, set up a time for them walk the property. The easier you can make this on the seller, the better. You don't want to scare the seller because you bring in ten people over the course of a week to view the house. Try to narrow it down to a handful at most and tell the seller that these are your partners, contractors or financial partners. Do NOT tell them that this is the end buyer.

After the buyers walk through the property, they will be able to present you a firm offer, and you can select which works best for you. The goal is to work with the buyer that presents the highest offer, as long as everything else is equal. For example, one buyer may make an offer that is $5000 higher, but if they take 30-days to close, you may be better working with the buyer that can close within 7-10 days. The name of the game is getting paid and working towards your next deal.

**Assigning the contract**

Once you have confirmed the offer and the deal is done, it's time to open escrow and get to the title agency. Again, make sure that your buyer can close in no more than 14 days, but hopefully less than 10. When you get to the title agency, the end buyer will open up escrow and to make sure they are serious buyers, request that they put down at least $5000 to start that process. As soon as the escrow process begins, all mortgages, liens or debts will be paid first. This is important to ask in the buying process because all debts should be built in to your offer to the seller. There is nothing worse than losing a deal because you didn't know they still owe money on the home.

If you are wondering which contract you should use, we will send you the exact agreement we have used to close over 1500 deals. Visit allinnation.com.

## Getting paid

As soon as all debts are paid off, the seller gets paid, you get your fee, and the buyer receives the deed to the house. The seller walks away free and clear, with cash in their pocket. You walk away with your check for all of your hard work, and the seller will gain a valuable asset. The title agency will handle the entire transaction and they will disperse funds via check or bank account wire.

## CHAPTER 9

# Starting Your Journey Towards Financial Freedom

There is a reason that over 90% of the world's millionaires have built their fortunes in real estate. There is also a reason why so many others get started and fail in pursuit of financial freedom. Real estate is tried and true, has a low barrier to entry, and opportunities are everywhere. However, this also means there is a lot of competition for those opportunities.

The preceding chapters show you the exact blueprint that helped us achieve wealth. If you follow the steps laid out in the book, you will be equipped with every skillset you need to land your first deal, and many deals after that. Real estate isn't rocket science, and once you perfect the scripts and processes you now know, it's now about mastering your craft. You will need to spend hundreds of hours making cold calls, talking to sellers, walking properties, and making offers. We highly encourage you to push yourself outside of your comfort zone and challenge yourself to make mistakes in pursuit of improvement.

You can only learn so much by reading books. Real mastery of any craft requires application.

Mike Tyson said it best, "everyone has a plan until they get punched in the mouth."

Spending hours rehearsing your script is essential, but nothing can prepare you like real-life experience. So many entrepreneurs get caught in the planning phase of their business. We often hear, "Once I practice my script, I'll make the calls," or "if I only had an extra $100, I could buy bandit signs."

If you have decided to make the leap, your excuses no longer matter. You can lie to your peers and say things are happening. You can tell everyone in your circle that you are "making moves." None of that matters anymore because you have jumped into entrepreneurship and only results will get you paid. The only way to get results is to take massive action in pursuit of your dreams. Once you change your mindset and understand that it's all about results, you will lock in on income-producing activities.

Once you start focusing on income-producing activities, you will begin to see progress in the form of mistakes. When you start making phone calls, you will mess up your script and lose a sale. That is progress. Once you get your first appointment, you will walk the property and have no idea what to offer. That is progress. When you do finally make an offer, you will forget to close or make an offer that isn't accurate. That is progress. If you are continually moving forward and making mistakes, you are way ahead of the entrepreneur that spends weeks or months stuck in the planning phase. So many aspiring entrepreneurs know their script perfectly, but never make a cold call.

It's about taking massive action.

Real estate is a simple business to learn. The difficult part is the self-mastery and the ability to persevere when times get tough. Every day there are hungry, well-seasoned professionals that are trying to take the deals that you are searching for. There will be plenty of times where you think you have a deal closed, and something doesn't go as planned. When that happens, understand what went wrong and stay connected to our success formula. Eventually, if you keep moving forward, the deals will come, and your life will change forever.

If you take nothing else away from this book, remember the success formula we discussed at the beginning of the book. This success formula will inspire you through the tough times and keep you focused on what matters.

## Step 1: Change your mindset

What are the stories you are telling yourself about your life right now? The only limitations that exist in this world are the ones you tell yourself. If you defend your limitations, you get to keep them.

If you are telling yourself "if only I had…" or "I can't make it because.." then you shouldn't start in real estate yet. You should spend all of your energy on personal development and lifting those self-limiting beliefs. There is not an excuse or circumstance that we haven't proven wrong. Sal Shakir grew up in a war zone, moved to America with nothing, and could barely speak English. Show me your current situation, and we will show you hundreds of people that came from worse situations to thrive and reach their dreams.

Who are the people you are spending the most time with? What are the conversations you are having with yourself?

The conversations you have with yourself and the ability to break free from your self-limiting beliefs will ultimately determine your success. If you can't truly convince yourself that you can be successful, how will you convince sellers or future employees?

You must make a conscious decision to change and accept full responsibility for your circumstance and success: no more half commitments or convenient excuses. Excuses are for employees that are trying to survive and maintain a steady paycheck. Your excuses won't help you once you decide to start your journey towards financial freedom and entrepreneurship.

Change your internal and external circumstances, and success will follow. All of the scripts, rebuttals, and systems we have given you won't help you if you don't conquer your limiting beliefs.

### Step 2: Commitment

Once you change your limiting beliefs and shift your mindset towards success, and make success your only option. Remember the story of burning your ships? Burn all of your ships and commit to figuring it out, no matter how painful the problem is. Are you currently in debt? Great! Use it as fuel.

Did you have a seller back out right before closing? Awesome, you are making progress.

Once you want to succeed as badly as you want to breathe, you will become successful. It requires that burning desire, day after day, and month after month to reach success. Eliminate every excuse that comes up and decide that nothing will stop you from reaching your goals.

For us, we had no other options. We were broke, we didn't have a degree to fall back on, and we couldn't get a loan to help us get started. We had no other choice but to become successful, so we did whatever it took.

Maybe you do have other options. If you do, that could become your biggest downfall because there will be someone else like us that doesn't. The person that MUST succeed will always beat the person that would like to succeed.

Burn your ships, take massive action, and make success your only option.

**Step 3: Sacrifice**

If you have decided that success is the only option, you must be willing to sacrifice everything in pursuit of success. Sacrifice means no more Netflix and no happy hours for a while. Netflix will be there in a few years after you build a massive team and create time freedom. For now, every available minute should be dedicated to your success and mastery of your craft.

You will have family members and friends that question or mock your commitment. This will be your first test because it's difficult to "disappoint" the people you love the most. Remember, this is your life not theirs. If they genuinely love you, they will support you even if they don't understand you. If they don't support you, it's not that they don't love you. Your family members don't want you to fail, and they are just projecting their own self-limiting beliefs onto you.

You have broken down your own self-limiting beliefs, and you have a huge WHY that is pushing you to achieve greatness. If you want to become the 1%, you must be willing to accept that 99% of people won't understand you. That means you are on the right track because 99% of people don't achieve the level of success that you are committed to creating. Keep going and push beyond the naysayers. Once you are successful, they will be proud of you and will ask you how you did it. One of the most challenging hurdles when pursuing success is disappointing people around you. Saying no to friends and family will be hard at first, so make sure you remember your WHY.

Why do you want to be successful? Dig deeper than fancy cars or a Rolex watch. What truly inspires you to achieve massive success? If you are only working to buy a watch, you won't keep going once you purchase that watch. Your why could be your family, freedom or any deep foundational desire that will keep you going when times get tough. If your big WHY is to retire your mother, you won't stop pushing just because a seller was mean to you. Retiring your mom will always be your vision.

Once you know your WHY, the how becomes easy.

## Step 4: Execution

Steps 1-3 are vital for you to achieve success, but step 4 will save you a lot of time and headaches along the way. After you decide that success is the only option, you need to equip yourself with the right tools to get the job done. We have given you every script, strategy, and marketing option you need to land your first deal.

Now, it's about mastering those scripts, putting in the hours, and becoming an expert at your craft. Practice as much as you can, but don't forget; There are no replacements for action and experience. Give yourself permission to make mistakes and push yourself out of your comfort zone. If a cold call goes poorly, take a minute to understand what happened, practice that rebuttal and make another call. Real estate is a numbers game, and the people that become successful are the ones that make mistakes while moving forward.

Take the time to master your craft, invest in mentorship, and put systems in place for yourself right away. It will take some extra time in the beginning, but it will help you when it becomes time to teach your systems to your first employee. As you are learning and taking action, learn with intention to teach. Ask yourself "how would I teach this to someone else?" If you are learning with the intention to teach, you will master your craft and be able to scale once the deals start coming in.

Some practice until they get it right, but the best practice until they can't get it wrong.

**Step 5: Perseverance**

Real estate is the most simple yet complex industry in the world. We have given you every tool and resource you need to be successful, but undoubtedly there will be tests throughout your journey towards success. There will be days you want to quit and days where nothing seems to go right. Real estate isn't for everybody because most people can't handle the tough times. Alex Saenz spent month after month searching for deals and losing them along the way. He put in hours each day writing handwritten letters and bandit signs, and still nothing happened. Most people get deterred when they work hard but don't see results.

If you spend 80 hours per week searching for deals and make $0, will you quit? What if you do that for weeks or months and don't land your first deal? Most people will give up and quit. Alex didn't, and his perseverance has created generational wealth for his family. Most people quit just before they reach success, and that's what separates the successful people from those that wish they were successful.

Make sure your WHY is big enough and burn your ships. When times get hard, you can always go back to your why, and if you have no other options, you will figure it out no matter what.

## Closing

If you made it to the end of the book, you have already surpassed 80% of the people that bought this book. Did you know that 80% of books that are purchased don't get finished? It's a perfect analogy to show you what is possible if you decide to create the life of your dreams. Most people go their entire lives dreaming and planning the possibilities for their lives, but they don't make the commitment and sacrifice that will turn their dreams into a reality.

Has that been you? Are you always telling people what you are going to do, yet find an excuse when things get tough?

If that is you, don't beat yourself up over it. Up until now, you weren't in control. You were conditioned by friends, parents, teachers and self-limiting beliefs that held you back. Now, you're in control. You have made the conscious decision that success is not only possible; it's the only option. You changed the stories and programming inside your mind. You have committed to success and decided to take massive action. Next time a friend asks you to meet them for a beer, you have committed to yourself to sacrifice in the short term to reach your dreams. You understand your big why and have eliminated all of your possible excuses.

You have decided to become an expert at your craft by creating systems and daily success habits that match your massive goals. When all else fails, you have made the conscious decision to never quit on yourself and your why. There are no other options. You have no other choice but to succeed, and if you keep this message close to you, you WILL succeed.

Are you ready to change your life forever?

Are you ready to gain financial freedom?

Are you willing to go ALL IN?

Only you know the answer to those questions but just know, we believe in you.

## CHAPTER 10

# All in Prayer

**I am.**

I am the most powerful creation on earth.

I am capable of doing anything I set my mind to.

I am no longer a slave to limited beliefs.

I am chosen to break generational curses.

I am chosen to change the financial trajectory of my family's existence.

I am created to THRIVE not just survive.

I am created to be a person of extreme value.

I am created to be massively successful.

I am created so that once I am massively successful I can then serve others at the highest level.

I am.

I am the most powerful creation walking this earth and now it's time to maximize on my potential.

When I leave this earth I want to tell God that I used every single ounce of potential that was in me.

I am no longer scared.

I walk by faith.

Where there is faith, fear cannot exist.

I am and I believe!

I am and I believe!

I believe!

We want to wish you peace, love, happiness, abundance and success every day as you inspire others to do the same. God bless.

ALL IN NATION / Allinnation.com

Made in the USA
Thornton, CO
07/20/24 21:03:57

e1daf30a-e9fb-4f2d-90e7-faa301803e16R01